PERKINS&WILL
MIAMI
Twenty-Five Years

PERKINS&WILL
MIAMI

Twenty-Five Years

Foreword by Rodolphe El-Khoury
Interviews by Andres Viglucci
Edited by Oscar Riera Ojeda

OSCAR RIERA OJEDA
PUBLISHERS

Table of Contents

8   **Foreword**
by Rodolphe el-Khoury

10   **Introduction**
by Andres Viglucci

14   **Vision & Perspective**
Lawrence Kline

16   American Express Sunrise Corporate Center
24   Jackson West Medical Center Doral Campus
28   Confidential Energy Services Provider Florida Headquarters

36   **Design & Purpose**
Pat Bosch

38   Miami Dade College Academic Support Center
54   L'Oreal Research & Innovation Center
64   Princess Nourah Bint Abdul Rahman University
70   Core Wynwood

74   **Impact & Influence**
Jose Gelabert-Navia

76   Greater Accra Regional Hospital at Ridge
84   Baptist Miami Beach 709 Alton Road
88   CEMDOE: Centro Médico de Diabetes, Obesidad y Especialidades
96   Hebrew School

98	**Culture & People** Carlos Chiu	180	Glossary
100	Perkins&Will Miami Studio	186	Photography Credits & Captions
106	St. Stephen's Episcopal Day School Arts and Innovation Center	192	Firm Profile & History
		193	Studio Members
116	City of Sunny Isles Beach Gateway Center	194	Awards
		196	Publications
		200	Book Credits

126 Knowledge & Research
Jose Bofill

128 Ransom Everglades School STEM Building
144 Florida International University Academic Health Center Five
152 Broward College/FIU Miramar West Center

156 What's Next: Future Leaders
by Andres Viglucci

158 Jacksonville Landing/One Park Jax
162 Nicklaus Children's Hospital Advanced Pediatric Care Pavilion
168 University of Miami Student Village
172 Cisneros Group Miami Headquarters

Miami is rhythm and music, sun, wind, and water. It's unapologetic, bold, and opinionated. It floats on a river of grass and rises defiant above ten feet of porous rock. It's sea level rising and extreme events and drying aquifer, yet it remains optimistic and joyful and determined to survive and grow. The Miami Studio has embraced this city's diversity and resilience. For 25 years our work has explored and resolved the challenges given and the opportunities granted. Like our city, our studio thrives and builds on this journey of beauty, the human condition, and invention, framed by its rhythm, nature, boldness, artistic vibrancy, and passion.

Foreword
Rodolphe el-Khoury

Rodolphe el-Khoury is Dean of the University of Miami School of Architecture. Before coming to UMSoA in July, 2014, he was Canada Research Chair and Director of Urban Design at the University of Toronto, Head of Architecture at California College of the Arts, and Associate Professor at Harvard Graduate School of Design. He has taught at Columbia University, Rhode Island School of Design, and Princeton University and has had Visiting Professor appointments at MIT, University of Hong Kong, and Rice University (Cullinen Visiting Chair). After earning a Bachelor of Architecture and Bachelor of Fine Arts from Rhode Island School of Design, el-Khoury obtained a Master of Science in Architecture from MIT and his Ph.D. from Princeton University.

el-Khoury was trained as both a historian and a practitioner and continues to divide his time between scholarship and design. As a partner in Khoury Levit Fong (KLF), his award-winning projects include Beirut Martyr's Square (AIA San Francisco), Stratford Market Square (Boston Society of Architecture), and the Shenzhen Museum of Contemporary Art (AIA Cleveland). His books on eighteenth-century European architecture include *The Little House, An Architectural Seduction*, and *See Through Ledoux; Architecture Theatre, and the Pursuit of Transparency*. Books on contemporary architecture and urbanism include *Monolithic Architecture, Architecture in Fashion, States of Architecture in the Twenty-first Century: New Directions from the Shanghai Expo*, and *Figures: Essays on Contemporary Architecture*.

The Perkins&Will Miami Studio was the first start-up office conceived to serve the region as well as being a gateway to Latin America and international work. The studio grew organically with Jose Gelabert-Navia, Pat Bosch and an initial group of professionals from The City and other Perkins&Will studios. The Miami office quickly established itself as a presence in the City, through the strong connections Jose had in the community, Pat's design leadership and the firm's leadership commitment and collaboration.

The Miami Studio has evolved through the combined talents of a core group of individuals who have been with the Firm for many years, joining Jose and Pat and creating a strong culture and successful model of thought leadership and entrepreneurship, including Carlos Chiu, Jose Bofill and Lawrence Kline. A new generation of vibrant architects from all over the world has joined the team in the last decade, continuing the Studio's established tradition of quality and complexity.

The firm's buildings, which now constitute a substantial and highly praised portfolio, are easily recognized. The trained eye will see the characteristics of ever changing massing and planes that ingeniously align a distinctive aesthetic sensibility with climate responsibility.

The layperson will also recognize staples of the Miami Studio. These are the generous canopies, overhangs, public terraces, and urban rooms that overtly shape and carve buildings as receptacles for public life. Regardless of their function or site, these buildings prioritize and perform their civic mission literally and figuratively. Literally, by pulling the public realm from the street and extending it deep into the building in a sequence of communal space. Figuratively, with building forms that anticipate and assume the presence of the public, much like a door handle would imply a missing hand. The buildings are dedicated to the public and they are shaped by this dedication.

Take the Miami Dade College Academic Support Center, where a colossal canopy shades a roof terrace stretching the entire length of the structure. it is the culmination of a sequence of communal spaces that brings the street into the building and extends it up through a spectacular atrium—the social hub of the building.

The same observation holds for Baptist Miami Beach. The building invents a unique mixed-use healthcare experience for the neighborhood, It is reminiscent of urban infrastructure, with an elevated parking garage—an extension of the street—prominently exposed. An oversized canopy envelops the entire building, shading a roof terrace and an outdoor space of generous proportions. The environmental and symbolic logics align here: the canopy provides shade and mitigates passive solar heat gain. It also frames and monumentalizes the building's public rooms, offering them as civic space.

The transition from the street to the large urban rooms nested within the building is often the primary means of architectural expression. Consider for instance The greater Accra Regional Hospital at Ridge. Ramps and stairs are the dominant features here; they draw a sculptural map of how the public moves through and occupies the building. Together with the generously distributed terraces, roof gardens, and canopies, they constitute the building as a vertical extension of the public realm.

It is with these characteristic traits in mind that I think of the architecture of Perkins&Will's Miami Studio as a civic practice. Civic, not only because it specializes in public institutions but especially because of the attention the designers invest in the relationship between institutions and the public they serve. This attentiveness to the public defines the "brand." It is evident in the properties of the buildings themselves as much as in the values that they bring to their surroundings. In a variety of buildings designed for institutions locally and globally, Perkins & Will, is committing to an architecture that primarily provides and stands for the neighborhood and its community, from access to generous amenities to the expression of civic character.

The values and civic inclination that permeate the work can also be found in the makeup of the firm itself. The Coral Gables office is indeed reputed for being one of the most desirable and inclusive workplaces in Miami. Its culture is built on the same principles of generosity, community, and inclusion that are embodied in the built form.

The culture of the office also extends to external relations and to its rapport with the city. Perkins & Will has assumed a leadership role in Miami by supporting its institutions and especially its universities, including my own. It is with great pleasure and anticipation that I welcome this collection, long overdue, of works that have so generously served cities across the world and their citizens.

Introduction

Andres Viglucci

Andres Viglucci covers urban affairs for the *Miami Herald*. He joined the newspaper's staff in 1983 after a two-year stint at the Associated Press in New York and Miami. At the Herald, he was a key member of a team that won the Pulitzer Prize and the Goldsmith Prize for Investigative Journalism from Harvard's Kennedy School in 1999 for coverage of a fraud-marred Miami mayoral election. He was also a lead reporter on the Herald's Pulitzer-winning coverage of the saga of Cuban rafter child Elian Gonzalez in 2000. As urban affairs writer, he has written about planning, development, architecture, historic preservation and affordable housing in Miami, among other topics.

In 1996, architects Jose Gelabert-Navia and Pat Bosch, who met while teaching at the University of Miami, launched the Miami office of Perkins&Will, the storied Chicago firm.

The studio was, in essence, a start-up. There were no clients, no projects. But the timing seemed propitious both for Miami and Perkins&Will, then embarking on an ambitious expansion that would turn it into one of the world's largest design-focused architectural firms.

Miami, meanwhile, was just emerging from a tumultuous decade and a half that had seen race riots, the Mariel boatlift from Cuba, white flight and steady migration from Latin America and Europe dramatically remake the city's economy and population. But things were looking up: the South Beach revival was well under way, putting Greater Miami on the cusp of the latest and perhaps most consequential in a series of successive transformations that today have made the metro into a global cultural and economic polestar.

It wasn't an easy launch, though. Gelabert-Navia, for many years the studio's managing director and today regional director for Latin America, recalls having a "great" lunch with a prospective client, a local developer. At the conclusion, Gelabert-Navia confidently asked, "So, when do we start?" only to be "crushed" by the response, delivered softly with hand on shoulder: "Come back to me when you have something to show."

The work of course did eventually come. The first were two public high schools, commissions won in part through Perkins&Will's reputation for civic and educational design. Those were followed over the next several years by projects of increasing scale, prominence and sophistication as Bosch, Gelabert-Navia and the core team of home-grown leaders they assembled patiently built a creative and expansive studio culture, a deep store of experience and expertise, and a far-ranging global practice that marries science, technology and rigorous functionality to artistry and, explicitly and maybe unusually for a profession that sometimes seems to shy away from the word, beauty.

Now, a quarter century after its founding, the Miami studio of Perkins & Will has plenty to show for itself.

Its extensive portfolio exhibits a variety, complexity and design ingenuity that will thrill anyone who's paying attention, and people increasingly are—including clients old and new from around the world and at home in South Florida who seek out the Perkins&Will Miami studio for big, high-profile projects in higher and secondary education, in science and tech, in healthcare, and for sprawling corporate facilities.

Under Bosch, Gelabert-Navia and the rest of its five-person leadership—Managing Director Lawrence Kline, Operations Director Carlos Chiu and Science and Technology Practice Leader Jose Bofill—the studio has adroitly ridden the crest of the Miami wave, drawing on the city's multicultural milieu for talent and for lessons in how to collaboratively adapt, build and design for diverse cultures and environments at home and around the world.

Bosch, design director from the studio's inception, stresses that what made it all work was an early decision to establish the practice and its brand as a design office, making it a cornerstone for Perkins&Will as it expanded.

"It was winning and leading through design," Bosch says. "It was the vital piece."

Its challenging and successful projects in places as disparate and far-flung as Ghana, Kazakhstan and Saudi Arabia, where the Miami studio led the design of the world's largest university for women in 2009, have provided lessons and know-how for the office's newer projects for Florida International University and Miami-Dade College, Jackson Memorial Hospital and American Express, among many others. The results have helped raise the bar for South Florida civic and institutional architecture, pointing to better ways to conceive of and design college buildings, acute medical facilities, scientific labs and corporate offices so that they improve work, learning and life for the people who use them.

The clean, contemporary appearance of the studio's projects belies the considerable rigor and analysis, and the often mind-boggling functional and operational complexity, that underlie the studio's finished projects.

The Miami studio's buildings don't shout. There is no signature look. Every one of the buildings its architects produce show distinctive design moves, but they arise organically from a project's function and location. Environmental sensitivity is integral to every design. Orientation, passive shading devices and efficiency of materials and energy use are built in from the start of every job.

Bosch calls the studio's approach "purpose-driven design," a philosophy based on Perkins & Will's founding principles of humanistic design. Those human-centered tenets extend not just to projects and clients but to the studio workplace and its staff of around 60.

Steeped in inclusivity, mentoring and collaboration, the studio culture is reflected in an office plan where no one has a private office, walls and doors are fully transparent and furnishings can be reconfigured along with project teams, without rigid hierarchies of authority or disciplines.

Twenty-five years on, and counting, the Miami studio of Perkins&Will is a design practice with deep local roots whose reach, influence and reputation extend far across the world.

Vision & Perspective
Lawrence Kline Managing Director

Growing up in 1960s Miami Beach instilled Larry with a love for modernist architecture that would ultimately lead him to take a different professional path than his father and both of his brothers, who became real estate attorneys. Instead, he chose to follow his passion for art and design. The intersection of indoor and outdoor living in Miami helped to shape his design philosophy of following a simple palette. He strives to create designs that work in harmony with and enhance the natural environment by showcasing clean, strong architectural forms in tune with the landscape and the strength of natural light in a tropical environment.

Larry has spent his life living in the Miami area. After graduate school in New York and Florence, and a brief stint working in Washington DC, he returned to his roots in Miami understanding the growing importance of South Florida's architecture, art, culture, and wonderfully diverse community.

As the Managing Director of our Miami studio, Larry has taken a conscious approach to creating a culture of professionalism and inclusiveness inside of the office and outside in the design community. These tenets form the foundation of his viewpoint that respect and integrity are to be honored, nurtured, and protected.

"We want to grow through really great design and we want to grow through integrated design, where architecture, interiors and landscape are all around the table informing the project. I think it provides a richer design solution when people can cross disciplines and get out of their traditional roles."

Architect Lawrence Kline, Miami born and bred, never wanted to practice anywhere else. So after architecture school in New York state, he hightailed it back home, hoping to build on the rich legacy of Mid-Century Miami tropical modernism—a style not so revered then as it is now—that inspired him to become an architect.

"I love the city," Kline says. "I grew up in what I still think of as an amazing architectural context of Miami modernism in a tropical environment with amazing landscape. This palate of white architecture, blue sky and green landscape influenced me ever since I was a kid."

It may be subtle, but that architecture of place, and the possibilities it suggests for contemporary design, is an undeniable antecedent to the work of Perkins&Will's Miami studio. That all-in approach to a project, one where building exterior and interiors, landscape and environmental design are inseparable parts of a whole, is what Kline has been increasingly focused on since joining the practice in 2013, after 26 years as a design principal at Spillis Candela and Partners, the first homegrown Miami firm to do many things under one roof.

The Miami studio had been in business 15 years when Kline was recruited to join as managing director, one member of a leadership triumvirate that's standard in every Perkins&Will office, along with the design director and director of operations.

But the office's reputation had not yet caught up to its extensive portfolio of sophisticated projects at home and around the world, Kline said.

"I saw a studio that delivered really complex, beautiful design solutions that seemed to be under the radar in terms of visibility in South Florida," Kline recalled. "People didn't know about us."

Kline set himself an ambitious goal that soon set the office on a path to greater recognition: To undertake even bigger, better projects, growing in size and stature while preserving a nurturing studio workplace culture to support and retain talented designers and foster production of consistently distinctive architecture.

It's proven no easy chore, but you can't have one without the other, Kline says.

"The majority of the job is strategic thinking about how you have the studio thrive, deliver great design, and promote a culture of design collaboration and inclusion," he says. "How do you establish, promote and nurture an inclusive culture in a design studio? The vision and perspective is that that is a lot more difficult than it seems."

The effort has paid off, he said. And the proof is in the increasingly prominent educational, laboratory and educational STEM projects the studio has completed, both abroad and in its South Florida home. Embracing local cultural influences and ways of building that take the environment into consideration has served the studio well. Its designers know how to adapt because in Miami they have to, he says.

"I love the idea that we can export design talent and design," Kline says. "There is nobody better at delivering complex, lab-based science and STEM."

Kline takes special pride in the quality of design and conception of hometown projects like the new Jackson

West hospital, a branch of the public Jackson Memorial system in the fast-growing Miami suburb of Doral.

"I'm proud of the impact of our architecture. It enhances the fabric of South Florida, buildings that become beautiful objects that provide a quality of architecture and space," he says. "Jackson Hospital in Doral is an elegant, beautiful object sitting in a landscape in front of a water feature.

"But when you think about the complexity of medical equipment and MRIs and PET scanners and all of the shielding of walls from radiation that you have to do, they are complex buildings that are delivered in this very restrained, elegant manner. We do architecture that is technologically smart; on the cutting edge of skins and materials and energy conservation."

That intimate connection to the Miami community can only help the Miami studio keep on thriving, Kline said.

"Having seen the sine curve of Miami since I was a child, I honestly believe we're in the best of times for a city in terms of being a global attraction. People want to live in Miami, they want to come to Miami.

I love the evolution of where it's going, and we want to capitalize on that.

"The city has design firms that have come and gone. I think it's important to celebrate 25 years of a practice, and a practice that we will sustain for the next 25 years."

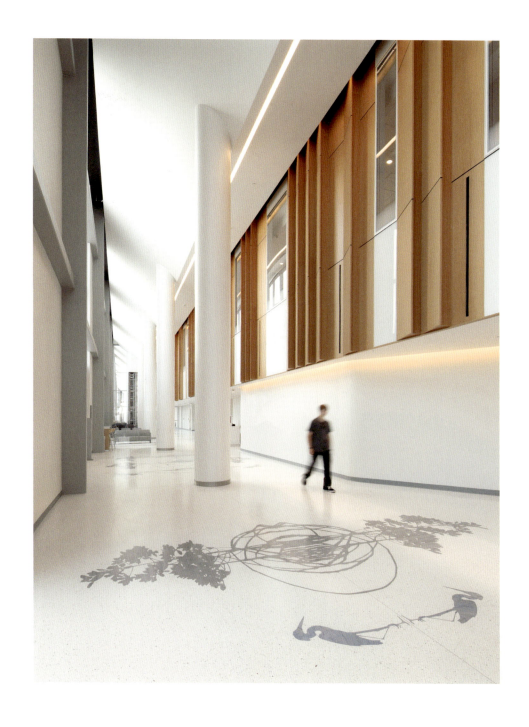

Design & Purpose
Pat Bosch Design Director

A founding partner of the Miami studio of Perkins&Will since 1996, Pat Bosch leads the office as its Design Director. Internationally recognized for her design acumen and collaborative work style, Pat routinely brings together diverse groups of stakeholders to generate ideas and find common ground; design solutions emerge out of the strong partnerships she builds with her clients. Pat takes a humanistic and environmentally responsible approach to design that is supported by research and meticulously executed process. She combines edgy creativity with careful examination of every project's program, context, region, and local culture to produce design solutions so innovative that they consistently challenge the status quo.

Her work has been honored with several national and international design awards, and has been featured in architectural magazines and industry journals around the world. The strength of Pat's design portfolio has made her a sought-after contributor to global forums, councils, commissions, and other architectural think tanks. In 2018 she spoke at the National Building Museum as part of the Spotlight on Design Series and was a key contributor to the Fast Company Innovation Festival in NYC. Pat brings a multicultural, multinational perspective to her practice.

Her fluency in four languages and ability to empathize with codes, customs, and beliefs around the globe—from the Americas and Europe to the Middle East and Africa—have allowed her to thrive in a variety of environments with a diverse range of clientele.

"The DNA of the Miami studio is the creative pursuit of purpose-driven design. There are opportunities that every project brings for transformation, for beauty, for change, for commentary, for innovation, for inspiration. We seek projects that can tell a story, have meaning, and become relevant parts of society."

While building a career with high profile firms in New York City, Pat found herself teaching at the University of Miami where she met Jose Gelabert-Navia and, making a life changing decision, helped launch the Perkins&Will Miami studio. Having never lived in Miami, she was drawn by the rare chance to build an architectural practice that suited her personal and professional philosophy.

At the Perkins&Will Miami studio, Bosch has found the space and support to develop a design culture focused on buildings and projects that "leave the world a better place." In doing so, she also helped define the parent firm's meticulous design process to fulfill the mission that the CEO outlined to her a quarter century ago.

"I fell in love with it, and my job was to propel that vision. It was a start-up, we had nothing," Bosch recalls. "It was like building your own firm with the parameters and the support of a firm with a legacy of design and civic leadership.

Now Bosch couldn't conceive of working anywhere else. She was the first female design director at Perkins&Will, and is to this day the only Hispanic woman—Bosch was born in Cuba—to hold the titles of design director and architecture design principal at the firm.

"Our firm and studio have trail-blazed in many ways," she says.

Bosch and Gelabert-Navia quickly realized that design quality could be the Miami studio's calling card. It wouldn't be an architecture of capricious gestures or star turns, but clean, contemporary and creative design based on thorough and rigorous research, the client's needs, and, in a "critical regionalist approach," tied closely to geographical and cultural context.

"The studio became an epicenter," Bosch says. "That's why we did a lot of international work from here. Because we could. We built it as a design studio because that's where our strength was."

The approach Bosch seeded in the Miami studio is open and collaborative. Mentoring is key. Principals, leaders and associates comfortably take on different roles on project teams that include landscape and interior architects as integral members, not afterthoughts.

The ultimate goal: to achieve unity and beauty of purpose and design through a merger of art, craft and science.

"Beauty is found at every moment," Bosch says. We should never take away beauty and the soul of a project from the history of design and architecture."

The studio has stressed quality of project over quantity, Bosch says. Especially appealing to her are "unclassifiable" projects that cross typologies and engender innovation to change lives.

In 2013, her team was responsible for the design of Saudi Arabia's massive Princess Nora Bint Abdulrahman University, the world's largest center of higher education for women, and an engine of change for the zealously conservative kingdom.

"It totally changed society. It's one of those things where Perkins&Will did their magic," she says. "When I walk into PNU, the sheer scale of it, the things we did there, were telling the story of the women of Saudi Arabia."

That experience of building elsewhere, of changing the way things are usually done, has in turn informed the studio's most recent Miami and South Florida projects. At the Jackson Memorial public health system's Jackson West medical center, the Miami studio helped administrators reconceive the look, feel and layout of a hospital and patient floors to make it more hospitable to the people who go for wellness and healing. To conceive a hospital as the heart of a community and a true civic center.

"When we were doing Jackson, it was not just another hospital. We were changing the way they were thinking. We were changing what a hospital is nowadays," she says. "It's a de-institutionalizing. They bought into the vision that you need to be a different model of community hospital, and Miami can lead the way.

"This studio really wants to put Miami on the map and do it in a very intellectual way. I think Jackson West is a unique version of a hospital. Design and purpose has to do with a sense of discovery and knowledge of a place and a program and a reason for it. Of coming to a realization that there is a bigger purpose to fulfill, delivering that with knowledge and research and information, and then creating beauty and a human experience.

"Those are the things that are inspiring and the engine for the expression of a new beauty and expression."

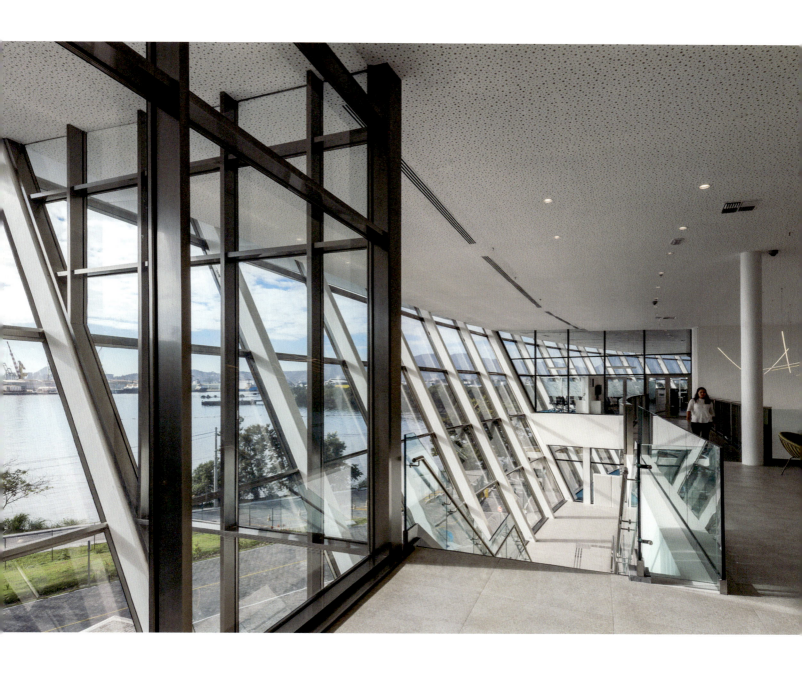

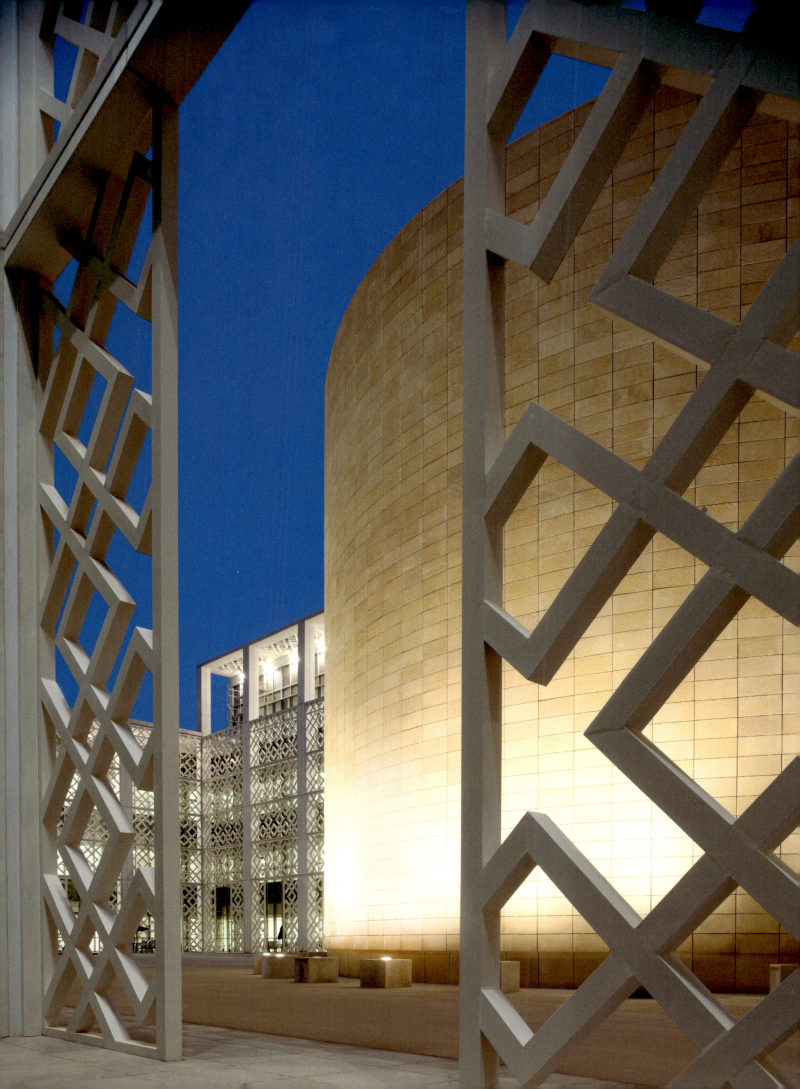

Impact & Influence
Jose Gelabert-Navia Principal

As the child of two architects, Jose was immersed in the world of architecture practically from birth. His earliest memories of life in Cuba and later of Puerto Rico, consist of driving around from building to building to visit their growing practice.

Exile from Cuba shaped the path of Jose's career. He developed a global curiosity, moving from country to country, learning from each new location. This experience afforded him a level of comfort when he made Miami his home—he found he could easily relate to all of the diverse cultures that make Miami so unique.

Jose has dedicated his career to projects with a positive social impact. When analyzing new opportunities, he asks how they can improve the quality of life for their future inhabitants. He measures a project's success by the relationship the user has with the facility. Just recently, Jose received photos of doctors, nurses, students, and patients enjoying the new Greater Accra Regional Hospital facility, a project he managed, and it is for this reason that he continues to stay driven to find meaningful work for the firm.

Jose previously held the position of Dean at the University of Miami's School of Architecture where he started the school's architecture program in Italy. He credits trips to Italy and other parts of Europe as being transformative to his career.

"We made a difference. For us, the greatest contribution originally in Florida was raising the level of K-12 and Higher Education. We came in when the universities were moving more and more to a research base, and we were able to contribute to that. We've also made a dent in Miami in terms of what we've been able to achieve as a Design Studio. Twenty-five years ago it was difficult to get people to come to work in Miami. Now we have the pick of the litter."

Jose Gelabert-Navia was working with his parents, both architects, in a small family firm in Miami when he got a call from a friend. Would he like to start a local office for Perkins&Will? Gelabert-Navia said yes, on one condition: that he could keep teaching at the University of Miami's architecture school, where he had been on the faculty since 1981.

A quarter century later, that connection to teaching and education remains a vital element in Gelabert-Navia's practice as an architect, and to the work of Perkins&Will's Miami studio, where he was Managing Director for fifteen years and remains a Principal. At UM, Gelabert-Navia today leads courses in Contemporary Latin American and World Architecture and teaches in the school's popular program in Rome, which he founded.

Gelabert-Navia credits a peripatetic youth—born in Cuba, he moved to Puerto Rico with his family as a young exile before attending architecture school in New York and settling in Miami—with stimulating a wide-ranging curiosity and an eagerness to learn from different places and cultures.

That's an attitude he sought to infuse in the studio's practice from its early days, and one he believes has been central to its growth and impact as the office sought and won coveted, competitive commissions both at home in multicultural, polyglot South Florida, and across Latin America and some off-the-beaten path places elsewhere around the world.

"I have always thought this is where the teaching comes in for me," Gelabert-Navia says. "One of the points I make to my students is, you have to understand the culture of a place. Buildings don't just exist independently of the culture that produced them.

"In Brazil, I would spend time talking with people who had nothing to do with us getting the project. That works with clients at a certain level. The fact that you know more about their culture than maybe they do breaks the ice, for otherwise why are they going to hire a firm from the United States?"

Back when he was helping launch the studio in 1996, Gelabert-Navia was challenged by a would-be client to come back to him in two years when they had work to show off.

And education was where Gelabert-Navia thought the local Perkins&Will office, which after all had been known for its design of schools since the 1930s, could make a name for itself. He assembled a team that included Pat Bosch, a UM colleague and the studio's Design Director from day one; Carlos Chiu, today Operations Director, and Jose Bofill, who had been a student at UM, as a young Associate.

They would grow together in the Miami studio and the profession, gaining knowledge and experience as they went along, initially with the backing of other Perkins&Will offices—first on public school projects, then on planning and design of university laboratories and academic buildings, each project building on the last.

"I said, 'We have to show what we can do,'" Gelabert-Navia recalls. "And we began getting better and better work in research, better and better work in healthcare."

That strategy—bringing in young architects, giving them rein to work on big projects, letting them grow on the job, encouraging them to set down roots in Miami—became a cornerstone of the practice's success, he says.

"The idea that someone can grow into their role and have a stake in Miami," he says. "I always thought in Miami you

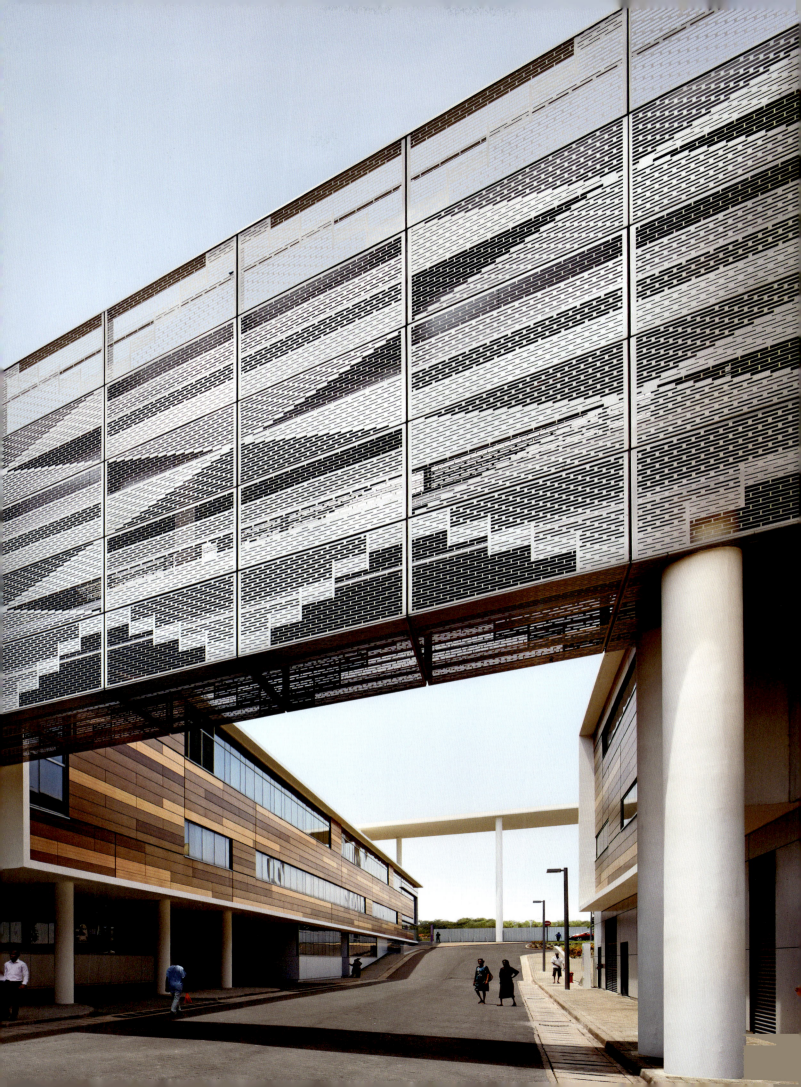

can write your own ticket. You have to have the talent, but you have to create your own opportunities. What I tried to do was create the right circumstances and recognize the substance everyone had."

The opportunities for work grew out of that homegrown approach. For instance, when French construction conglomerate Bouygues was looking for a firm to design a new, groundbreaking hospital in Ghana, its Miami subsidiary, Americaribe, suggested the local Perkins&Will office. Gelabert-Navia, who managed the project, recalls the sense of accomplishment he and his colleagues felt when they received photos of medical staff, students and patients at the newly inaugurated hospital.

What they learned on projects abroad then helped elevate their work at home in Miami and Florida as well. Significant educational projects in the office's portfolio range from science and classroom facilities at state universities and colleges in Miami, Tampa, Pensacola and Jacksonville to science buildings at local private schools and, now, a Hebrew school being built in Santiago, Chile.

The studio has also seeded South Florida's architectural landscape with some of its best architects and designers, who have become sought after by competitors for the skills and experience they acquired at Perkins&Will in Miami.

That, too, is proof of the studio's enduring impact and influence, Gelabert-Navia said—and its prospects for continued success at home and elsewhere.

"When we started this 26 years ago, if you said Perkins&Will, people would say that's a Chicago firm that does schools," Gelabert Navia says. "This certainly has come a long way from 'come back when you have something to show me.'"

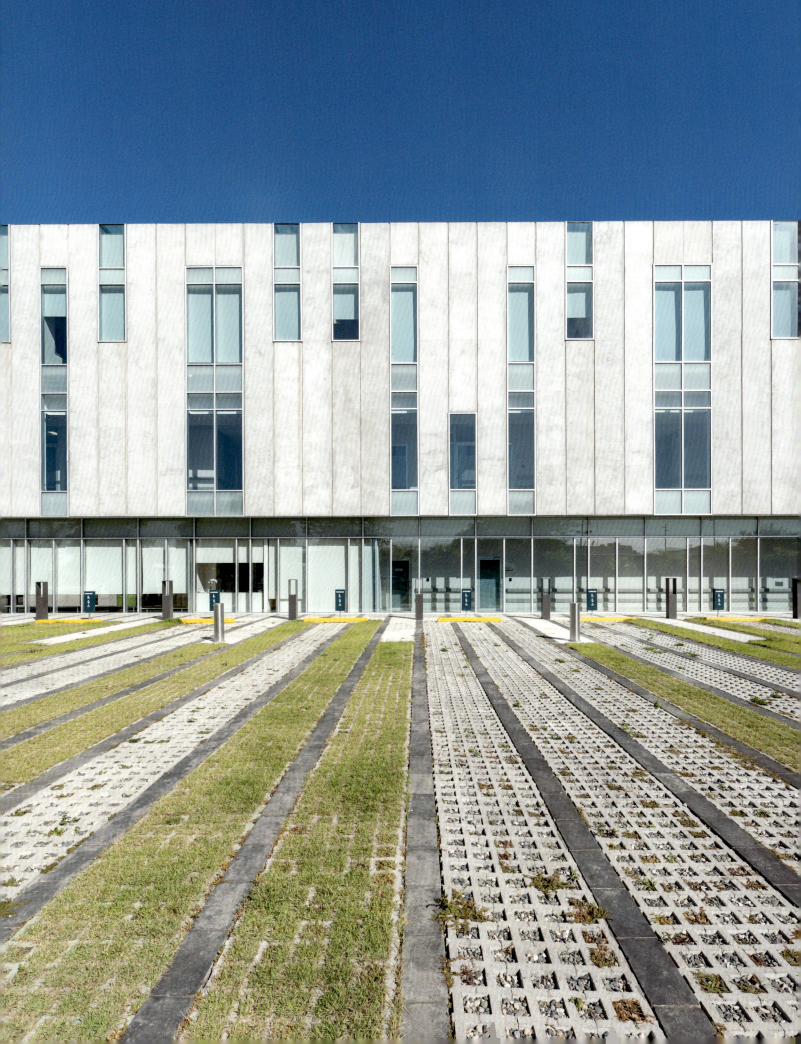

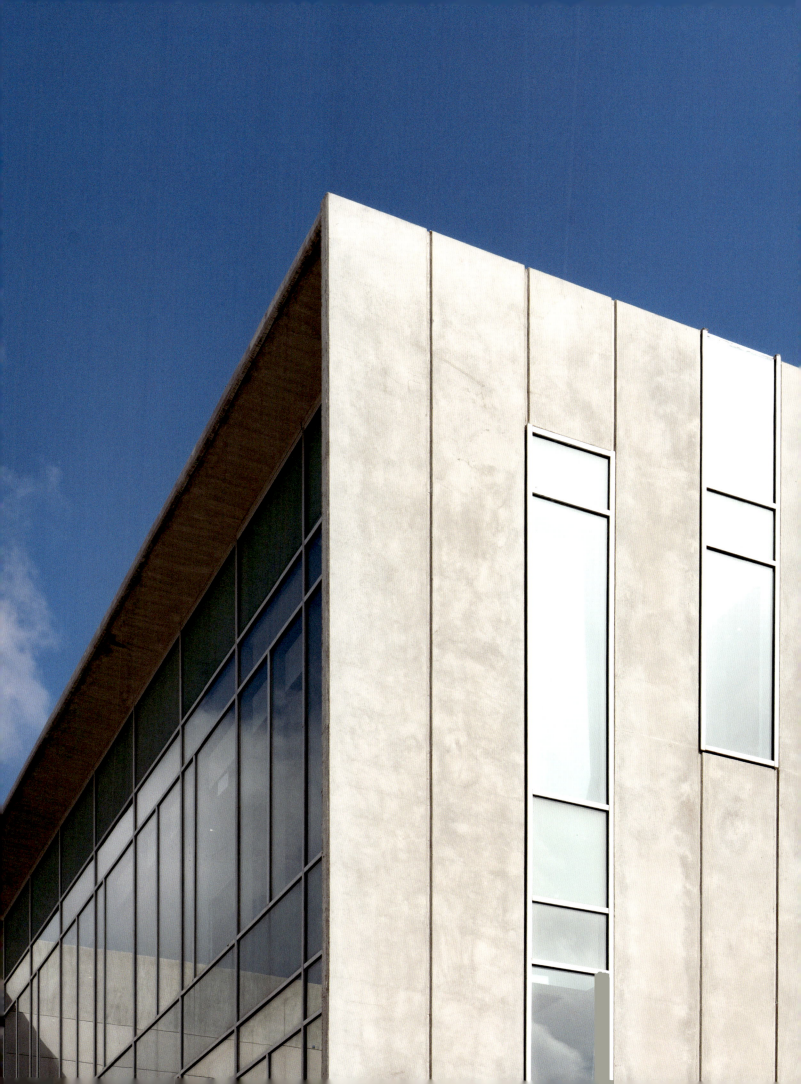

Culture & People
Carlos Chiu Director of Operations

Carlos prides himself on his ability to roll up his sleeves and finish tasks. His philosophy is based on hard work and consistency. His straight-to-the-point approach has led to the successful management of many of the Miami studio's largest and most successful projects.

After graduate school, Carlos spent time in Spain, France, and Peru. The experience of traveling abroad strengthened his love for architecture, its history and the materiality in buildings. A self-described "Jack of all trades," Carlos spends nearly all of his free time building millwork, taking on improvement projects, or tinkering with mechanics. His attention to detail and finely grained understanding of the construction process has helped him to navigate large-scale construction administration phases on a variety of project types.

Carlos lives in his projects, often staying engaged years after occupancy. His level of involvement during construction develops meaningful relationships with his clients. He acts as a client advocate, looking out for their best interests from big-picture design down to small material details.

> "Our culture, the way we treat people, the way we manage our teams, the way we support our staff and partners, for me that's really the most important part. We have a very diverse group of people here, and from just about everywhere. Everyone's welcome. We celebrate different cultures. It's about bringing your culture to the office, infusing and elevating who we are as people and designers."

Carlos Chiu's life and career path is, in many ways, the paradigm for the people who work at Perkins&Will's Miami studio.

Born in Cuba, he settled with his parents as a refugee in Spain before coming to Miami, where he was shaped and educated. An inveterate tinkerer adroit at several disparate skills, Chiu majored in business before going to architecture grad school at the University of Miami.

Chiu has spent a full 22 years of his 30-year architectural career at Perkins&Will in Miami, where, putting his business education to best use, he switched professional focus from design to finance and management.

As the Miami studio expanded, so too did Chiu grow into his role. For many years now, Chiu has been the guy who makes things happen. And he's been the architect of the Miami studio's warm, welcoming office culture. Like the multifaceted Chiu himself, it conjoins cultures and disciplines to promote personal and professional growth, and, ideally, a long tenure at the studio.

Today, a third of the Miami studio's staff of around 60 was born somewhere other than the United States. And numerous members of the studio workforce have been with the office for more than a decade. That's not by accident, Chiu says.

"I'm supposed to be the financial guy," Chiu says. "But my primary thing has been to try to ensure, as much as we strive for perfection and excellence and innovation, that the culture of the office from a humanistic standpoint is upheld. We prefer to have young people come to work here and have them grow here. Most of the leadership group has grown up here. Someone like me is very typical of our senior leadership.

"A lot of people are here partly because of that. We're always talking about family as much as you can be a family in an office environment. This office is very different from other corporate-based offices. One of the reasons we've been able to survive is that we've been a Miami office with a corporate structure, and not trying to shove a corporate structure into a Miami office. Miami is a cultural melting pot, and so are we."

That's not to say the studio's designers aren't pushed or challenged, Chiu says. They are. But everyone gets the guidance and opportunity to hone and expand skills and knowledge, filling different roles on project teams to broaden their experience and instill versatility and flexibility—hallmarks of the studio.

"We want to make sure we have a well-rounded staff. You're never relegated to doing one thing and repeating it through five projects because you're really good at it," Chiu says. "It feels like school here sometimes. We do research like it's a design class. We feel this is your doctorate, your next-level degree. If people leave, I want them to be the best architect across the street. When we pursue work, one of the words we look for is 'fun.' Having a passion for something, enjoying it, being proud of it. As much as we create a good culture here, people are here for the projects."

Under the exacting process developed by the Miami studio's founding director of design, Pat Bosch, those who ultimately benefit the most from the office culture are the clients, who almost always get much more than they bargained for, Chiu says.

"Pat drives it beyond financial parameters to deliver the best we can," Chiu said. "We surprise our clients time and again. We're giving them more than they ever hire us for."

And the results are what matters in the end. It's why so many talented people stick with the Miami studio of Perkins&Will.

"We have a very hard time letting go of anybody," Chiu says. "If we hire somebody, we want them to work for us forever. That's the goal."

Knowledge & Research
Jose Bofill

A South Florida native, Jose Bofill finds a feeling of "home" far beyond the four walls of a house. The designer spent most of his childhood outdoors, surrounded by lush greenery and the wide expanse of the Atlantic Ocean—and he believes design and technology can work together to protect this home.

Jose grew up in a creative family, and his grandmother, a painter and sculptor, instilled a sense of wonder and curiosity in him from a young age. He discovered his passion for architecture in its mix of technical potential and artful expression, and has been investigating that connection for over 20 years with our Miami studio. His projects are not only beautiful, but technically advanced and always designed with the future of the environment in mind.

Miami's subtropical climate is one of the most unique in the U.S., and so is its culture. By bringing his creative skill as well as his family's Cuban heritage to the studio with him every day, Jose is deeply rooted in Miami culture and intimately familiar with the local environmental challenges that the city faces. Under his leadership, the studio has focused on supporting cross-cultural connections in the community and integrating sustainability into the very core of the design process.

"The simple solutions tend to be the most powerful, the most effective. An approach informed by research arms us with the knowledge to solve the design problem in an elegant but simple way. We are a contemporary design firm, embedded and rooted in research. We will continue to evolve and progress around that."

Jose Bofill was an undergraduate at the University of Miami when he began moonlighting for Perkins&Will's new Miami studio, building architectural models. Though hesitant to work for a large corporate firm, he joined the small, fledgling Miami practice two years out of school, persuaded that it offered the best of both worlds.

"What I was told by Perkins&Will was that we would be a small office, but would have the national firm behind us," Bofill recalls. "That was very intriguing."

Just how intriguing Bofill would soon find out, when, with but a scant few years of professional experience under his belt, he was flung into the architectural cauldron as project manager for the office's first commissioned science laboratory, a biomedical research facility to be designed and built at Florida Atlantic University in Boca Raton.

The learning curve was steep, but Bofill and the Miami studio had the backing of Perkins&Will's Atlanta office, where science and technology were the practice's forte. That FAU lab launched Bofill and the local studio on a path to becoming one of the leading planners and designers of science and technology buildings for schools and corporations, not just in Florida, but in the U.S. and abroad.

At first, the Miami studio relied on the extensive expertise of Perkins&Will. Today, other Perkins&Will offices turn to Bofill and the Miami studio for the font of knowledge and experience they have accrued and refined over more than two decades, and the striking project designs that arise from it.

"I have had the opportunity to work with almost every office at Perkins&Will. We built the Miami studio by collaborating, by bringing in and developing that knowledge and expertise, coupled with design excellence," Bofill says. "We leveraged the firm portfolio to gain the expertise, and now we are leveraging our own projects."

Every project at the Miami studio begins with intensive research as the basis for innovation and design, expanding the office's already broad foundation of knowledge and experience. As environmental sustainability has come to the forefront, that's come to also mean investigations of building materials like high performance glass and glazing systems for managing heat and glare, as well as healthy indoor air and non-toxic materials, Bofill says.

"That is our purpose: to have sustainability built into our practice, guided by a framework we call Living Design."

The approach underpins the Miami studio's increasingly hybrid designs, which seamlessly blend programs and elements from different areas of science and technology, healthcare, education, corporate workplace, and hospitality design to humanize them. That research-first approach has enabled the office's architects to creatively tackle projects in a wide range of countries, cultures and environments, Bofill says.

That means science and medical education projects in countries as different as Kazakhstan, which experiences extremely high and low temperatures, and Brazil, where the studio was responsible for an ecologically friendly research lab on Rio de Janeiro's Guanabara Bay for French cosmetics giant L'Oreal.

"It does allow us to go into different parts of the world and understand them culturally and climatically," Bofill says. "We draw from that research to inform the design. Not just for science and tech, it's for all the practices. It's critical to our practice. Our clients come to us because of our

knowledge and the research that we do, and how that transfers into our designs."

At Miami's Florida International University, for instance, the Miami studio's design for an academic health center building provided an object lesson to both students and faculty in how science can inform other fields. The project team had to contend with a harsh south-facing exposure, so designers devised a sweeping façade of window boxes with unevenly shaped edges that act as static self-shading devices as the sun moves across the building.

"As the provost told us, 'You're designing for science with science,' Bofill recalls. "We're using scientific methods to design this façade, and it was a science building.

"One of our greatest successes in 25 years is that we've taken that knowledge and research to deliver locally and independently, and now we are exporting that knowledge and expertise."

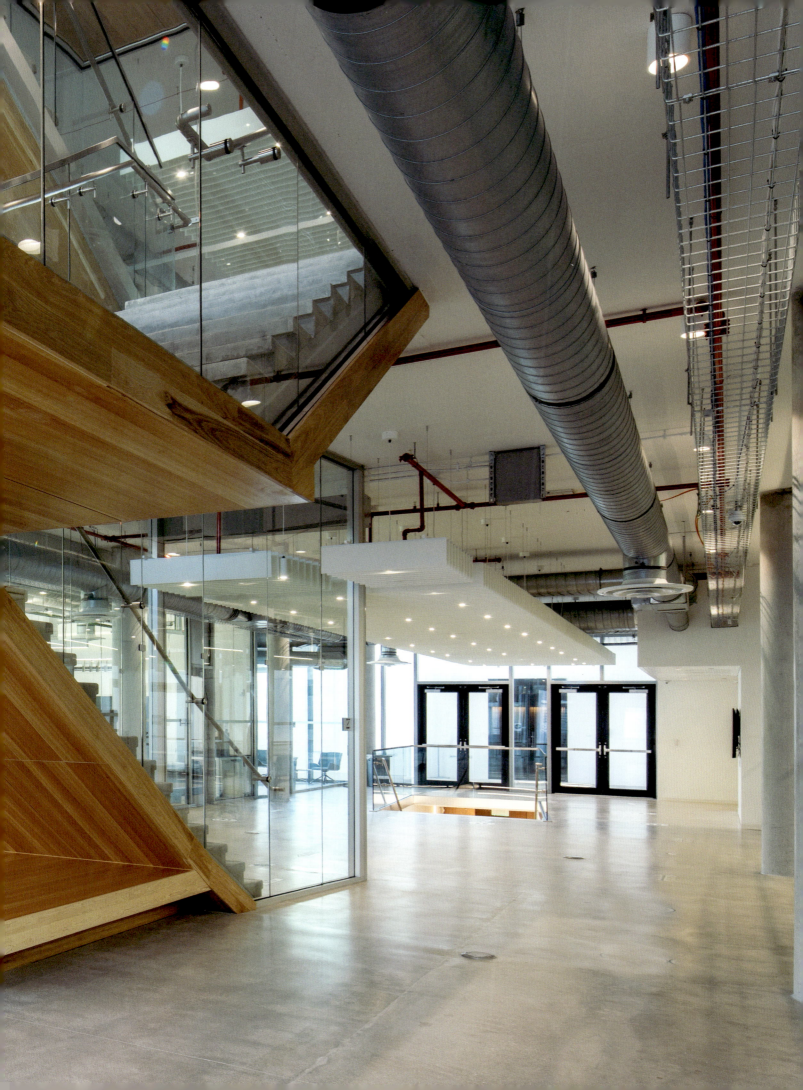

Looking Forward, a Conversation

Andrés Viglucci

Lincoln Linder
Adriana Portela
Kricket Snow
Angel Suarez
Fred Zara
Associate Principals

"In the time that I've been in Miami, we've seen a huge change in the attitude of ownership of clients, in the public interest, and a lot more value placed on design and architecture. Every year, I feel the prospects get better and better, and the more that we can engage with those kind of clients and build for them, I think the closer we are to getting the right kind, the best kind of work, the work where we can have the greatest impact." – Angel Suarez

In hindsight, it's clear the launch of the Miami studio of Perkins&Will in 1996 came at a perfect time. The city, poised to surge, subsequently underwent a quarter century of sometimes tumultuous growth and transformation. The studio, in remarkably parallel if smoother fashion, grew and developed along with it.

Now, as the studio heads into its next 25 years, Miami is in the midst of yet another of its metamorphoses, one that's spawning building projects at an ever-larger, ever-more ambitious World City scale. And no one's better positioned to take that on than the Miami practice.

The rank of associate principals, with tenures at the studio ranging from eight to sixteen years, represents its future. And its members stand ready and eager to extend and cement the studio's growing standing, impact and influence at home in South Florida, across Latin America and anywhere else in the world where clients come calling—always with the keen emphasis on design that has been the studio's hallmark from the start.

Lincoln Linder, joined in 2006
"When I joined Perkins&Will, the Miami studio was half the size that it is today and we've been growing ever since. During the past twenty years there has been a critical mass of cultural development in South Florida and we've had the opportunity to be part of that cultural growth through partnerships with many of South Florida's most established institutions and businesses."

"Since we have completed such a broad variety of project types, we're uniquely positioned for the future. Programs have become more and more hybridized. Workplace and Healthcare have been infused with hospitality planning concepts. Education programs have also become more hybridized as flexibility, adaptability and team-based learning have become more important drivers in educational curricula. We are, therefore, positioned to take on any kind of project whether it exists today or has yet to be imagined."

Adriana Portela, joined in 2010
"The quality of the work we do here and the opportunities to work on complex project types is unique in South Florida. When you're committed to this kind of purposeful work, when you're committed to design, there is nowhere else to be.

"I've never worked on a project where I'm not learning. And not just in increments, but in big leaps. It can be difficult and requires a lot of stretching outside of your comfort zone, but you never stagnate. We are at this springing-off point where we are working on a lot of high-quality work and clients are coming to us for that. It's an exciting moment.

"Another thing that excites me as a minority woman is seeing the firm evolve from an inclusion standpoint. When I think about all the amazing women we've been hiring, and they're all powerhouses, we hope they'll be part of the future leadership and that we are creating the conditions for them to grow into those roles.

"I hope to see more diversity in our principals' group. The firm is constantly looking at how we can improve, how do we recruit from more diverse universities, and how do we retain that talent?

"You have the ability to evolve at Perkins&Will, and as your career evolves you can change your focus. I don't

see a time where I'm not involved in design and delivery but my focus will start to adapt at some point to more mentorship and shoring up of the next generation. Right now, we're still in the thick of it. We're learning and we're pushing and growing with each project."

Kricket Snow, joined in 2014
"What I am so appreciative of is that the teams and people I have worked with on every project have been outstanding, professionally but also such a pleasure to work with. There's a group that has been here 12 years, for 20 years. There is a solid core.

"In my career, I have not been pigeonholed in any particular project type. I think that's what keeps me motivated. I'm constantly learning. Our office allows those of us who are generalists to continue to cross boundaries. At the root, design is about human behavior. It's about how people use the space and about psychology and sociology and interaction. That is the common thread that connects us to our projects.

"I certainly see myself staying here until the end of my career. I would be happy in any leadership role where I have the opportunity to contribute in a meaningful way.

"Being able to work on projects that are impactful, and that have intent, and allow us to have some fun is inspiring. I'm a big believer in office culture. We spend so much time here that working with people you want to work with, and having some levity, and having a good time even though you're working like crazy, is important, it's healthy."

Angel Suarez, joined in 2007
"I was born and raised in Miami. So this is my hometown. I've seen this city morph so many times. I love the fact that it's always changing and that it's become so much more diverse over the years, and that we're a city that craves that diversity.

"For the studio, the big shift in the work happened when we started on the Princess Noura Bint Abdul Rahman University project. We changed scale quickly and significantly. We went from single buildings to dealing with a whole complex at scale, but also collaborating in a much richer way, a seamless way. I think that was a turning point for our office.

"Anything related to that kind of civic and cultural work would be the most important for us to go after. I feel like we would very much enjoy being involved in that, being able to explore some things that we haven't yet been able to explore. Our work is characterized by large civic-type spaces, even if they're not necessarily civic projects—atriums and grand soaring spaces, light-filled spaces.

"In Miami, the building culture has changed, the economics have changed. It continues to expand and get closer to a global city status in terms of the budgets, in terms of the aspirations. We've definitely been trying to move the needle since we've been here, working with whatever we have to advance our discipline, the architecture of our city and the tropics as a whole.

"I think it's a great moment to be here. It's a great moment to be where we are, to have built what we've built so far and to continue to build on that."

Fred Zara, joined in 2016
"We want to be changing and improving people's lives. Since I have been at Perkins&Will, and especially here in Miami, I have always been surprised at how, even with a smaller team, we're able to deliver complex and large-scale projects.

"We want to be leading projects that will affect how you go day by day, living in a city. We want to be engaging in the public realm, with a larger impact on society or communities. So, civic and cultural work, anything that would affect how one spends one's days living in a big city like Miami—projects with that kind of public outreach, would be a priority for us.

"Of course, because Miami is having this moment, there's a lot of attention and a new group of players interested in being here. I think that, as a design firm, we need to position ourselves in a smart way so that we can take advantage of those opportunities, but without changing the way in which we have learned to grow in the past, which is naturally and gradually.

"As designers, we are always looking for new things to learn and new experiences to have. Even in the few years that I've been in Miami, one can perceive the changes the city is going through. With that, we get new challenges, new opportunities."

Glossary
1996-2022

1996

Diagnostic Treatment Center
Location: Miami, Florida
Client: Jackson Memorial Hospital
Size: 300,000sf

1997

St. Agatha Chapel
Location: Miami, Florida
Client: St. Agatha Catholic Church
Size: 100,000sf

1999

Madorsky Residence
Location: Miami Beach, Florida
Client: Madorsky
Size: 6,200sf

School of Communication
Location: Coral Gables, Florida
Client: University of Miami
Size: 57,000sf

2000

Caribbean Technology Center
Location: Guaynabo, Puerto Rico
Client: Caribbean Technology Center
Size: 200,000sf

2001

Winterhaven Hotel Restoration
Location: Miami Beach, Florida
Client: Coral Beach Hotels and Resorts
Size: 60,000sf

2002

Village of Merrick Park Offices
Location: Coral Gables, Florida
Client: Rouse Company
Size: 500,000sf

School of Aviation
Location: Homestead, Florida
Client: Miami Dade College
Size: 36,000sf

Charles E. Schmidt, Biomedical Research Facility
Location: Boca Raton, Florida
Client: Florida Atlantic University
Size: 90,000sf

Hotel Victor
Location: Miami Beach, Florida
Client: Zom, Inc.
Size: 96,000sf

Cypress Bay High School
Location: Weston, Florida
Client: School Board of Broward County
Size: 320,000sf

2003

Bacardi USA Headquarters Concept
Location: Miami, Florida
Client: Bacardi
Size: 110,000sf

Robert Morgan Education Center
Location: Miami, Florida
Client: Miami Dade County Public Schools
Size: 265,000sf

Delray Beach Public Library
Location: Delray, Florida
Client: City of Delray Beach
Size: 50,000sf

2005

Miami Institute for Age Management & Intervention
Location: Miami, Florida
Client: Medical Institute for Age Management
Size: 9,000sf

Interdisciplinary Research Building
Location: Tampa, Florida
Client: University of South Florida
Size: 140,000sf

2006

Clinical Research Building and Wellness Center
Location: Miami, Florida
Client: University of Miami
Size: 426,000sf

FAU/HBOI Marine Science Partnership
Location: Ft. Pierce, Florida
Client: Florida Atlantic University
Size: 43,500sf

American Airlines Admirals Club A
Location: Miami International Airport
Client: American Airlines
Size: 9,500sf

Bayview Market "Big Box Retail"
Location: Miami, Florida
Client: BDB Miami, LLC
Size: 625,000sf

2007

Platinum on the Bay
Location: Miami, Florida
Client: Maysville, Inc.
Size: 950,000sf

3333 Biscayne Boulevard
Location: Miami, Florida
Client: Cardinal Development
Size: 335,500sf

Brickell Financial Center
Location: Miami, Florida
Client: Foram Development
Size: 750,000sf

2008

806 Douglas Road Studio
Location: Coral Gables, Florida
Client: Perkins&Will
Size: 7,700sf

2009

Miami Jewish Home for the Aged
Location: Pembroke Pines, Florida
Client: Jewish Home for the Aged
Size: N/A

Life Science and Technology Park
Location: Miami, Florida
Client: University of Miami
Size: 1,800,000sf

School of Education
Location: Coral Gables, Florida
Client: University of Miami
Size: 72,000sf

Medical Discovery Institute at Lake Nona
Location: Orlando, Florida
Client: Sanford-Burnham Presbyterian
Size: 180,000sf

Torrey Pines Institute for Molecular Studies
Location: Port St. Lucie, Florida
Client: Torrey Pines Institute
Size: 102,000sf

Princess Nourah Bint Abdul Rahman University
Location: Riyadh, Saudi Arabia
Client: Dar Al Handasah
Size: 30,000,000sf

City Hall Annex
Location: Miami Beach, Florida
Client: City of Miami Beach
Size: 300,000sf

Signature Place Mixed-Use Development
Location: St. Petersburg, Florida
Client: Gulf Atlantic Real Estate Companies
Size: 884,500sf

2010

Campus Master Plan Update
Location: Miami, Florida
Client: Florida
International University
Size: 7,000,000sf

Sarasota Technical High School
Location: Sarasota, Florida
Client: Sarasota County Schools
Size: 320,000sf

2011

Hospital Universitario, San Vicente de Paul
Location: Rionegro, Columbia
Client: Hospital Universitario
Size: 53,000sf

2012

Advanced Biological Sciences Building
Location: Jacksonville, Florida
Client: University of North Florida
Size: 116,000sf

Academic Support Center
Location: Miami, Florida
Client: Miami Dade College
Size: 135,000sf

Clinical Translational Research Building (CTRB)
Location: Gainesville, Florida
Client: University of Florida
Size: 120,000sf

2013

Science Classroom Complex, Academic Health Center 4
Location: Miami, Florida
Client: Florida
International University
Size: 137,000sf

Stempel Complex Academic Health Center 5
Location: Miami, Florida
Client: Florida International University
Size: 119,000sf

2014

Mirarmar West Center
Location: Miramar, Florida
Client: Broward College & Florida International University
Size: 89,000sf

University of Miami
Location: Coral Gables, Florida
Client: University of Mimi
Size: N/A

2015

Sunrise Corporate Center
Location: Sunrise, Florida
Client: American Express
Size: 1,343,000sf

Hajj City
Location: Medina, Saudi Arabia
Client: Ministry of Finance
Size: 4,850,000sf

Ras Abu Abboud
Location: Doha, State of Qatar
Client: Municipality of Doha
Size: 170,700sm

2016

Advanced Pediatric Care Pavilion
Location: Coral Gables, Florida
Client: Nicklaus Children's Hospital
Size: 215,000sf

Hospital Universitario
Location: Chihuahua, Mexico
Client: Intelhealth Group of Monterrey
Size: 30,000sm

2017

The Greater Accra Regional Hospital at Ridge
Location: Accra, Republic of Ghana
Client: Bouygues Construction
Size: 465,500sf

Kuwait University
Location: Kuwait City, Kuwait
Client: Kuwait University
Size: 1,200,000sf

Luxury Automotive Showroom & Offices
Location: Miami, Florida
Client: Confidential
Size: 1,200,000sf

L'Oréal Research & Innovation Center
Location: Rio de Janiero, Brazil
Client: L'Oréal
Size: 142,500sf

School of Medicine
Location: Astana, Kazakhstan
Client: Nazarbayev University
Size: 405,000sf

2018

First Year Student Village
Location: Coral Gables, Florida
Client: University of Miami
Size: 482,000sf

ED/OR Expansion
Location: Deerfield, Florida
Client: Broward Health
Size: 75,000sf

Ras Matbakh Waterpark Hotel
Location: Doha, Qatar
Client: Confidential
Size: 350,000sf

709 Alton Road
Location: Miami Beach, Florida
Client: Baptist Health System
Size: 120,000sf

2800 Ponce De Leon Miami Studio
Location: Coral Gables, Florida
Client: Perkins&Will
Size: 13,700sf

Hebrew Institute
Location: Santiago, Chile
Client: Estadio Israelita / Instituto Hebreo
Size: 33,713sm

Confidential International Private K-12 School
Location: Miami, Florida
Client: Confidential
Size: 145,000sf

Bahia Urbana
Location: San Juan, Puerto Rico
Client: Government of Puerto Rico
Size: 97 acres

2019

Overtown Cultural and Entertainment District Master Plan
Location: Miami, Florida
Client: Simkins Industries
Size: N/A

930 Washington
Location: Miami Beach, Florida
Client: Simkins-Finvarb, LLC
Size: 88,500sf

Columbus Senior Living
Location: Columbus, Ohio
Client: Big Rock Partners
Size: 349,550sf

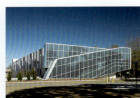
Laboratory Sciences Annex
Location: Tampa, Florida
Client: University of West Florida
Size: 53,000sf

2020

Miami Headquarters
Location: Miami, Florida
Client: Cisneros Group
Size: 24,500sf

STEM Building
Location: Miami, Florida
Client: Ransom
Everglades School
Size: 45,000sf

Puerto Polanco Mexico
Headquarters
Location: Mexico City, Mexico
Client: American Express
Size: 137,000sf

1212 Lincoln Road
Location: Miami Beach, Florida
Client: Crescent Heights
Size: 141,500sf

2021

Cayman International School
Location: Grand Cayman,
Cayman Islands
Client: CIS
Size: 146,000sf

Fortress Transportation & Infrastructure (FTAI)
Miami Office
Location: Miami, Florida
Client: Fortress
Investment Group
Size: 6,500sf

Jackson West Medical Center Doral Campus
Location: Doral, Florida
Client: Jackson Health System
Size: 605,000sf

Arts & Innovation Center
Location: Miami, Florida
Client: St. Stephen's Episcopal
Day School
Size: 25,000sf

Gateway Center
Location: City of Sunny
Isles Beach
Client: City of Sunny Isles Beach
Size: 17,000sf

Confidential Energy Services Provider Palm Beach Garden Headquarters
Location: Palm Beach
Gardens, Florida
Client: Confidential
Program: 2,000,000sf

Vox Miami
Location: South Miami, Florida
Client: TREO Development
Size: 373,000sf

Centro Médico de Diabetes, Obesidad y Especialidades (CEMDOE)
Location: Santo Domingo,
Dominican Republic
Client: CEMDOE
Size: 80,000sf

2022

Core Wynwood
Location: Miami, Florida
Client: Goldman Properties
Size: 115,000sf

Engineering Center
Location: Miami, Florida
Client: Florida
International University
Size: 126,000sf

One Park Jax
Location: Jacksonville, Florida
Client: Jacksonville DDA
Size: 6 acres

Surgical Tower
Location: Miami, Florida
Client: Nicklaus
Children's Hospital
Size: 215,000sf

Photography Credits & Captions

Photography by
Robin Hill.

Photography by
Steve Hall.

Photography by
Steve Hall.

Photography by
James Steinkamp.

Photography by
James Steinkamp.

Photography by
Robin Hill.

Photography by
Robin Hill.

Photography by
Robin Hill.

Photography by
Perkins&Will.

Photography by
Perkins&Will.

Photography by
Perkins&Will.

Photography by
Perkins&Will.

Photography by
Robin Hill.

Photography by
Robin Hill.

Photography by
Robin Hill.

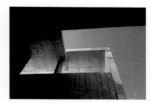

Photography by
Robin Hill.

Photography by
Robin Hill.

Photography by
Robin Hill.

Photography by
Robin Hill.

Photography by
Robin Hill.

Photography by Robin Hill.

Photography by Robin Hill.

Photography by James Steinkamp.

Photography by James Steinkamp.

Photography by James Steinkamp.

Photography by James Steinkamp.

Photography by James Steinkamp.

Photography by James Steinkamp.

Photography by Bill Lyons.

Photography by Bill Lyons.

Photography by Bill Lyons.

Photography by Perkins&Will.

Photography by Perkins&Will.

Photography by Mark Herboth.

Photography by Mark Herboth.

Photography by Mark Herboth.

Photography by Mark Herboth.

Photography by Robin Hill.

Photography by Robin Hill.

Photography by Gustavo José Moré.

Photography by Gustavo José Moré.

Photography by Gustavo José Moré.

Photography by Gustavo José Moré.

Photography by Perkins&Will.

Photography by Robin Hill.

Photography by Robin Hill.

Photography by Robin Hill.

Photography by Robin Hill.

Photography by Robin Hill.

Photography by Robin Hill.

Photography by Robin Hill.

Photography by Robin Hill.

Photography by Kris Tamburello.

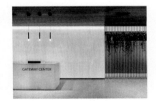
Photography by Kris Tamburello.

Photography by Kris Tamburello.

Photography by Kris Tamburello.

Photography by Kris Tamburello.

Photography by Robin Hill.

Photography by Robin Hill.

Photography by Robin Hill.

Photography by Robin Hill.

Photography by Robin Hill.

Photography by Robin Hill.

Photography by Robin Hill.

Photography by Robin Hill.

Photography by Robin Hill.

Photography by Robin Hill.

Photography by Robin Hill.

Photography by Robin Hill.

Photography by Robin Hill.

Photography by Robin Hill.

Photography by Perkins&Will.

Photography by Perkins&Will.

Photography by Miami in Focus.

Photography by Miami in Focus.

Photography by Miami in Focus.

Photography by Miami in Focus.

Photography by Perkins&Will.

Photography by Perkins&Will.

Photography by Kris Tamburello.

Photography by Robin Hill.

Photography by Kris Tamburello.

Photography by Robin Hill.

Photography by Robin Hill.

Firm Profile & History

Perkins&Will was founded in 1935 in Chicago, Illinois by two recent graduates from Cornell University, Larry Perkins and Phil Will. Larry's father, Dwight, was already a noted architect in the Mid-West with a reputation for the design of schools. The firm was started on the strength of an initial commission for the design of a new elementary school in Winnetka, Illinois, which they completed with the great Finnish architect Eliel Saarinen, who had recently migrated to the United States.

In the next fifty years the firm grew to over six hundred architects in two offices, Chicago, and White Plains. In 1987, Perkins&Will was acquired by the DAR Group, the world's largest privately held engineering/architecture company. DAR realized that the days of the mammoth centralized office, removed from the context that it served, was over. The new order was of a network of smaller studios made up of individuals who felt an allegiance to their region and would have a stake in the continued resilience and relevance of their work with a say in the running and wellbeing of their local team. In 1996, Perkins&Will started a strategy of national expansion to a network of offices across North America and beyond. The Miami studio of Perkins&Will was one of those original outposts. Founded by Jose Gelabert-Navia and Pat Bosch, it started with a staff of seven which has now grown to nearly seventy. From the outset, the office made a mark by winning work in many different sectors, from healthcare to education, and from science and technology to civic and corporate projects. Of particular pride to our team has been the continuity of many of the people behind its success. Unlike several other international shops that tried to set up in Miami to take advantage of the continuous cycle of boom and bust, Perkins&Will has been in continuous practice since inception. Our studio has grown and flourished as one of the main design studios in the region and as part of Perkins&Will's global presence.

This success was established early on by over 20 years of dedication and leadership from Carlos Chiu, Jose Bofill, Mark Lutz, and George Valcarcel. Ten years ago, Lawrence Kline joined this leadership group and became the new Managing Director, leading now with a larger group of remarkable professionals like Adriana Portela, Kricket Snow, Angel Suarez, Elina Cardet, Tatiana Guimaraes, Lincoln Linder, and Christopher Counts. Our Miami Studio portfolio and reach has evolved to encompass projects across the globe in over 18 countries, across all practice types. Our diverse studio is uniquely poised to deliver at the highest caliber of design and innovation, with a diverse group of creatives and experts from 12 different countries and with experience from the most prominent design backgrounds in the industry.

We look forward to a bright future and an exciting next quarter century with a firm foundation built on our legacy of work and many individuals who have made this achievement possible. We remain committed to our clients and our communities now and into the future.

Studio Members

Gustavo Alfonso · Javier Alonso · Vivian Alonso · Yovanna Alvarez · Soledad Amarante · Elizabeth Arias · Carlos Arredondo · Cynthia Atoui · Jon-Paul Bacariza · Anna Baez · Sarah Baquero · Jose Barcelona · Tara Beck · Francisco Bejarano · Ernest Bellamy · Jose Bernal · George Betancourt · Emily Bielen · Robert Bistry · Krista Blackburn · Celina Bocanegra · Jose Bofill · Adrian Bonnin · Pat Bosch · Alejandro Branger · German Brun · Yenny Calabrese · Michael Callahan · Alexander Camps · Jacqueline Candela · Elina Cardet · Karen Carmenate · Rodrigo Carrion · Brian Carson · David Cerame · David Chamberlain · Sara Chapman · Jovany Chediak · Carlos Chiu · Ligia Cisneros · David Cochran · Ryan Coffield · Heather Cohen · Giselle Coujil · Christopher Counts · Maria Counts · Dean Cretsinger · Kathryn Davis · Marisa Demontreiul · Robert Dennis · Yainie Diaz · Jose Diaz · Jason Dunham · Elieser Duran · Jean Felio Estabine · Zuleika Estevez · David Evans · Esther Ezzeldine · Marjorie Fallat · Ling Fan · Luis Fernandez · Ludovico Ferro · Michael Figueredo · Robert Fornataro · Allen Fuller · Isis Fumero · Rocio Galindo · Nick Garate · Daniel Garcia · Cesar Garcia-Pons · Nicollette Gasson · Jose Gelabert Sr. · Jose Gelabert-Navia · Werner Gilles · Eli Goldman · Jenny Gonzalez · Lilia Gonzalez · Denise Gonzalez · Julian Gonzalez · Melinda Graves · Jesse Guerra · David Guerrero · Julio Guillen · Tatiana Guimaraes · John Gustin · Ana Gutierrez · Carolina Gutierrez Lacayo · Irene Hegedus · Silvana Herrera · Karl Hirschmann · Ruben Hung · Brianna Hunter · Nora Hurtado · Yoka Ikourou · Etai Imna · Maria Iturriaga · Yulesis Izquierdo · Rose-Marie Javier · Hanna Jin · Silvia Junco-Fernandez · Ann Kistinger · Lawrence Kline · Lorena Knezevic · Maria Kontopanteli · Cynthia Kriz · Arely Lago · Mabel Lanza · Yongsug Lee · Crystal Lee · Virginia Li · Carlos Lima · Mandy Lindabury · Lincoln Linder · Marlene Liriano · Robert Lloyd · Jesse Lockwood · Alana Lopez · Mark Lutz · Sihui Ma · Ana Marin · Douglas Martin · Tatiana Maschi · Mary Matos · Lourdes Mayorga · Benjamin McGuirl · Giovanni Medina · Gustavo Mendoza · Irina Mitina · Tomasz Modzelewski · Alexander Montes · Young Moon · Mayra Mora · Juan Mullerat · Leslie Naghib · Jennifer Natareno · Juan Tomas Nunez · Gisel Orizondo · Neyda Otero · Jessica Pace · Gilbert Padron · Gergana Panteva · Christopher Park · Jorge Perez · Manuel Perez-Trujillo · Richard Perlmutter · Jorge Pernas · James Phillips · Ana Pirondi-Ibarra · Damian Ponton · Adriana Portela · Nilo Puentes · Camila Querasian · Miguel Quismondo-Garcia · Ali Qureshi · Carlos Ramirez · Jose Ramos · Ruben Ramos · Sunny Reed · Alba Reguero · Diana Reyes · Rod Reyes · Armando · Rigau · Belen Rivero · Hamed Rodriquez · Angelica Romero · Luciana Ruiz · Kelly Ryan · Gaston Saboulard · Jasmine Sadigh · Andrea Sandoval · Manuel Santana · Glen Santayana · Erica Schiff · Lindsay Shapiro · Dana Shores · Luis Silva · Kricket Snow · Hector Solis · Luis Sousa · Ryce Stallings · Laura Stevens · Rachael Stitzel · John Strasius · Lara Strasius · Jie Su · Angel Suarez · Zaima Suarez · Sandra Suarez · Tomoaki Sugimura · Susana Susana Rizo · Laura Swakon · Elizabeth Torres · Armando Urbisci · George Valcarcel · Carlos Vilato · Amanda Villa · Xiao Wang · James Wells · Juan Yactayo · Giannina Zapattini · Frederico Zara Chiarelli

Awards

2000
Educational Design Excellence, FAU Charles E. Schmidt Biomedical Research Facility, American School & University Magazine

2002
Award of Excellence in Architecture, Miami Dade College School of Aviation, AIA Miami Chapter

2003
White Ribbon Award of Merit, FAU Charles E. Schmidt Biomedical Research Facility, Florida Educational Facilities Planners Association (FEFPA)

2004
Excellence in Construction, Cypress Bay High School, Associated Builders & Contractors
Educational Design Excellence, Miami Dade College School of Aviation, American School & University Magazine

2005
Unbuilt Design Award, City of Miami Beach City Hall Annex, Society of American Registered Architects (SARA)
Design Awards Finalist, City of Miami Beach City Hall Annex, AIA Miami Chapter
Barbara Capitman Award for Excellence in Historic Preservation, Hotel Victor, Miami Design Preservation League
Design Awards Finalist for Restoration/Renovation, Hotel Victor, AIA Miami Chapter
Healthcare Environments Award - Health and Fitness Winner, MIAMI Institute for Age Management and Intervention, Contract Magazine
Design Awards Finalist Interior Design, MIAMI Institute for Age Management and Intervention, AIA Miami Chapter
Unbuilt Award of Merit, Platinum on the Bay, AIA Florida Chapter
Award for Outstanding Special-Use Building Design, University of South Florida Interdisciplinary Research Building, National Association of Industrial and Office Properties (NAIOP)

2006
Merit Award for Unbuilt Work, City of Miami Beach City Hall Annex, AIA Florida Chapter
Interior Designer of the Year Award, Marlene Liriano AIA Miami Chapter
Healthcare Project Design Forum Award, MIAMI Institute for Age Management and Intervention, IIDA Florida Chapter

2007
Educational Design Excellence, Academy@998, American School & University Magazine
Merit Award for Unbuilt Work, Bayview Market, AIA Florida Chapter
Institutional Project Design Forum Award, Gordon Center for Research in Medical Education, IIDA Florida Chapter
Interior Design Award of Merit, Gordon Center for Research in Medical Education, AIA Miami Chapter
Educational Design Excellence, University of South Florida Interdisciplinary Research Building, American School & University Magazine

2008
Best Unbuilt Design Award, 3333 Biscayne Boulevard, Society of American Registered Architects (SARA)
Best Built Institutional Design Award, Miami Dade College School of Aviation, Society of American Registered Architects (SARA)
Go Green Business Winner, Perkins+Will, Coral Gables Chamber of Commerce
Best Health Care, Torrey Pines Institute for Molecular Studies, Southeast Construction

2009
Excellence in Construction, Eagle Award, Institution $50-$99 Million, Sanford-Burnham Medical Research Institute at Lake Nona, Associated Builders & Contractors

2010
Award of Excellence for Unbuilt Design, Brickell Financial Centre Phase II Study, AIA Miami Chapter
Merit Award for Unbuilt Work, FIU Science Classroom Complex, AIA Florida Chapter
Award of Excellence for Unbuilt Design, FIU Science Classroom Complex, AIA Miami Chapter
Merit Award of Excellence for Renovations & Additions, Perkins+Will Miami Office, AIA Florida Chapter
Award of Excellence for Interior Design, Perkins+Will Miami Office, AIA Miami Chapter
Award of Excellence, Sanford-Burnham Medical Research Institute at Lake Nona, AIA Orlando
Award of Merit for Sustainable Design, Sanford-Burnham Medical Research Institute at Lake Nona, AIA Orlando
LEED NC Project of the Year - Large Building Class Award, Sanford-Burnham Medical Research Institute at Lake Nona, USGBC Central Florida Chapter
Award of Excellence for Green Building, Sanford-Burnham Medical Research Institute at Lake Nona, AIA Miami Chapter
Award of Excellence for Unbuilt Design, UF Clinical Translational Research Building, AIA Miami Chapter
Shortlisted for Future Projects - Health, UF Clinical Translational Research Building, World Architecture Festival

2011
Honorable Mention - Inspirational Award for Social Responsibility in Commercial Interior Architecture, YMCA Allapattah Family Branch, Contract Magazine
National Design Award of Honor, University of Florida Clinical Translational Research Building, Society of American Registered Architects (SARA)
National Design Award of Recognition, Florida International University Science Classroom Complex, Society of American Registered Architects (SARA)
Merit Award for Excellence in Architecture, City of Miami Beach City Hall Annex, AIA Miami Chapter
Merit Award for Unbuilt Work, Florida International University Science Classroom Complex, AIA Florida Chapter
Design Excellence/Commissioned Project, SANDI Award, Hospital Universitario San Vicente de Paul (Rio Negro), IIDA South Florida Chapter
Honorable Mention - Excellence in Hospitality Design, SANDI Award, Infinity at Brickell, IIDA South Florida Chapter
Shortlisted for Future Projects - Education, Princess Nora bint Abdulrahman University for Women, World

Architecture Festival
Longlisted - Interior Design Award, Hospital Universitario San Vicente de Paul (Rio Negro), World Architecture News
Award of Honor, Florida International University Campus Master Plan, The American Society of Landscape Architects, Florida Chapter

2012
Design Excellence/Commissioned Project, SANDI Award, Miami Children's Hospital Critical Care Tower & Emergency Room Expansion, IIDA South Florida Chapter
Honorable Mention - Design Excellence/Commissioned Project, SANDI Award, Zubi Advertising, IIDA South Florida Chapter
Design Excellence in Healthcare Design, SANDI Award Hospital Universitario San Vicente de Paul (Rio Negro) IIDA South Florida Chapter
Professional Design Firm of the Year, SANDI Award, IIDA South Florida Chapter
National Design Award, Zubi Advertising, Society of American Registered Architects (SARA)
Honorable Mention - Healthcare, Best Interiors, Hospital Universitario San Vicente de Paul (Rio Negro), IIDA Latin America
Longlisted - Healthcare Award, Hospital Universitario San Vicente de Paul (Rio Negro), World Architecture News
Award of Excellence, Signature Place, AIA Miami Chapter
Merit Award for Architecture, Residential Category, Signature Place, AIA Tampa Chapter
Honorable Mention - Healthcare, Best Interiors, Hospital Universitario San Vicente de Paul (Rio Negro), Contract Magazine

2013
Excellence in Architecture, Merit Award, University of Florida CTRB, AIA Miami Chapter
Excellence in Architecture, Honor Award, Miami Dade College Academic Support Center,AIA Miami Chapter
Unbuilt Design Honor Award, L'Oreal Research and Innovation Facilities, AIA Miami Chapter
Honor Award for New Work, Miami Dade College Academic Support Center, AIA Florida Chapter

2014
Merit Award of Excellence Greater Than 50,000 sf, FIU Stempel Complex, AIA Miami Chapter
Honor Award for Sustainable Design, UF Clinical Translational Research Building, AIA Florida Chapter
Honor Award for Unbuilt Design, Accra Regional Hospital, Ghana, AIA Florida Chapter
Merit Award of Excellence, FIU AHC 4, AIA Florida Chapter
Future Health Project, Accra Regional Hospital, Ghana, Design + Health International Award

2015
Honor Award for New Work, Broward College Southwest Center, AIA Florida Chapter
Award of Merit, Broward College Southwest Center, ENR Southeast
Honorable Mention in Higher Ed/University, FIU Science Classroom Complex, PCI Design Awards
Shortlisted for Future Projects, L'Oreal Research and Innovation Facilities, WAF
Pending announcement, Architectural Review
Pending announcement, WAN
Firm of the Year, Perkins + Will Miami Office, AIA Miami Chapter

2016
Honor Award for Unbuilt Design, L'Oreal Research and Innovation Facilities, AIA Florida Chapter
Honor Award of Excellence Greater Than 50,000 sf, Princess Nora bint Abdulrahman University for Women, AIA Miami Chapter
Hospital Design of the Year, The Greater Accra Regional Hospital at Ridge, Africa Health Summit

2017
Honor Award for Unbuilt Design, Ras Abu Abboud Doha, AIA Florida Chapter
Merit Award for New Work, The Greater Accra Regional Hospital at Ridge, AIA Florida Chapter
Honor Award of Excellence Greater Than 50,000 sf, The Greater Accra Regional Hospital at Ridge, AIA Miami Chapter
Honor Award of Excellence Greater Than 50,000 sf, American Express Sunrise HQ, AIA Miami Chapter
Sustainable Infrastructure Grand Prize, L'Oreal Research and Innovation Facilities, Green Solutions Awards

2018
Education Architectural Awards, Outstanding Project, Miami Dade College Academic Support Center, Learning By Design
Special Mention, Office Mid-Rise (5-15 floors), American Express Sunrise HQ, Architizer A+ Awards
The World's Most Innovative Companies in Architecture, #2, Perkins and Will, Fast Company
Best Healthcare Large Project, NICKLAUS Children's hospital Advanced Pediatric Care Pavilion, IIDA Miami
IIDA 2018 Healthcare Design Awards Transformation & Innovation Award, The Greater Accra Regional Hospital at Ridge, IIDA Healthcare Design Awards
The Top 50 Firms, 15th, Perkins and Will, Architect Magazine
Merit Award, Architecture Greater Than 50,000 sf, L'Oreal Research and Innovation Facilities, AIA Miami Chapter
Top 300 U.S. Architecture Firms, #2, Perkins and Will, Architectural Record
Giants 300, Top Architecture Firms, #2, Perkins and Will, Building Design + Constructions (BD+C)
Honor Award, Unbuilt Award, First Year Student Village, AIA Miami Chapter
Young Architect of the Year, Adriana C. Portela, AIA, AIA Miami Chapter

2019
Honorable Mention in the Spaces, Places, and Cities, L'Oreal Research and Innovation Facilities, 2019 World Changing Ideas Awards (Fast Company)
Highly commended for Healthcare Design (over 25,000 sqm), The Greater Accra Regional Hospital at Ridge, European Healthcare Design
Shortlisted for WAF, The Greater Accra Regional Hospital at Ridge, World Architecture Festival
Shortlisted for WAF, Hebrew School, World Architecture Festival
Finalist for Concepts - Plus - Architecture, The Greater Accra Regional Hospital at Ridge, Architizer A+ Public Voting

Corporate Small Projects, Less than 20,000 sf, Perkins and Will Miami Studio, Bragg Awards, IIDA Miami
People's Choice Award Top 5, 709 Alton Road, AIA Florida Chapter
40 Under 40, Gia Zapattini, Building Design + Simple Construction
Merit Award of Excellence, Nicklaus Children's hospital Advanced Pediatric Care Pavilion, AIA Florida Chapter
Honor Award, First Year Student Village, AIA Florida Chapter
Award of Merit, Neighborhood Planning Award, Coconut Grove Village Core Master Plan (Coconut Grove Business Improvement District), APA Florida
ARCHMARATHON Awards Miami 2019, Baptist Health Miami Beach Project 709, ARCHMARATHON Awards
Women in Architecture | Leadership Breakfast: October 4, 2019
Pat Bosch, AIA NY
The Excellence Award for Implementation, Coconut Grove Village Core Master Plan (Coconut Grove Business Improvement District), Gold Coast Section, Florida Chapter of the American Planning Association (local chapter)
Hospitality Design 2019 Women in Design Honoree, Pat Bosch, Contract Magazine
AIA Miami President's Award, Neyda Otero, AIA Miami Chapter
Honorable Mention in the Unbuilt Commercial Category, The Confidential Energy Services Provider Headquarters, Architecture Newspaper: Best of Design Awards
Editors' Pick for Commercial Office, American Express Sunrise Corporate Center, Architecture Newspaper: Best of Design Awards
BRAGG Award Best Corporate Design (Small SF), Perkins and Will Miami Studio, IIDA South Florida Chapter
Merit Award of Excellence Interior Architecture, NICKLAUS Children's hospital Advanced Pediatric Care Pavilion, AIA Miami Chapter
Honor Award of Excellence Interior Architecture, Perkins and Will Miami Studio, AIA Miami Chapter
Top 40 Healthcare Design Giants, #1, Perkins and Will, Interior Design Magazine
Top 100 Interior Design Giants, #2, Perkins and Will Interior Design Magazine

2020
Honor Award of Excellence, Interiors, Perkins and Will Miami Studio, AIA Florida Chapter
Award of Excellence, New Work, L'Oreal Research and Innovation Facilities, AIA Florida Chapter
Architizer A+ Public Voting, First Year Student Village, Architizer A+ Awards
Architizer A+ Jury Award, Unbuilt Institutional, First Year Student Village, Architizer A+ Awards
Honor Award for new Work, University of West Florida (Building 58 Lab Annex), AIA Northwest Awards
BRAGG Awards, Honorable Mention, Corporate Medium, Cisneros Headquarters, IIDA South Florida Chapter
Honor Award of Excellence, Interior Architecture, Cisneros Headquarters, AIA Miami Chapter
Honor Award of Excellence, Unbuilt Project, Hebrew School AIA Miami Chapter
Top Honor - Award of Excellence in Parking Structure Design, 709 Alton Road, Florida Parking and Transportation Association (FPTA)
Award of Excellence in Parking Structure Architecture, 709 Alton Road Florida Parking and Transportation Association (FPTA)

2021
Award of Merit, 2800 Ponce Plaza, FLASLA (Florida Chapter, American Society of Landscape Architects)
CAACE Project of the Year Award, JHS West Project, CAACE – Cuban American Association of Civil Engineers
Project of the Year, Honorable Mention, Gateway Center, IIDA South Florida Chapter, BRAGG Awards
Award of Merit, Unbuilt Category, 2800 Ponce Plaza, Florida Chapter American Society of Landscape Architects (FLASLA)
Award, Best Government Category, Gateway Center, IIDA South Florida Chapter, BRAGG Awards
Architecture Greater than / Merit, CEMDOE, AIA Miami Chapter
Architecture Less than / Merit, Ransom Everglades, STEM Building, AIA Miami Chapter
Honor Award of Excellence Interior Architecture, Gateway Center
AIA Miami Chapter
Best K-12, Ransom Everglades, STEM Building, PCI Design Awards

2022
FEFPA, FIU Engineering
A+ Awards Special Mention in the Primary & High Schools Category, Ransom Everglades, STEM Building, Architizer A+ Awards
A+ Finalist in the Hospitals & Healthcare Category, JHS West Project, Architizer A+ Awards
Honor Award for Unbuilt Work, Core Wynwood, AIA Florida Chapter
Merit Award of Excellence, Interiors, Cisneros Headquarters, AIA Florida Chapter
Shortlisted for WAF, Core Wynwood, World Architecture Festival (WAF)
Shortlisted for The Future Glass Prize, Core Wynwood, World Architecture Festival (WAF)

Publications

Building Design+Construction, "Private faculty offices are becoming a thing of the past," June 2022
Designer Spotlight Series, "Pat Bosch Finds Magic and Meaning in Design," March 2021
Arquitexto, "CEMDOE," March 2021
Arch Daily, "The Women of Perkins&Will Designing the Architecture of Tomorrow," March 2021
Fast Company, "This reimagined school takes a page from corporate America," February 2021
Modern Luxury Miami, "New Jackson West Medical Center Campus Set to Open in The City of Doral," January 2021
Modern Luxury Miami, "Miami's 30 Most Influential People," October 2020
Arch Daily, "L'Oréal Innovation Center," May 2020

Library of Congress, Pat Bosch Oral History, November, 2019

Ascent Magazine, "Florida International University Projects, Miami: FIU uses Precast Concrete to Build a Resilient and Beautiful Campus", Winter 2019

Redshift by Autodesk, "Is the Rooftop Architecture Renaissance a Fad or a Fixture", October 2018

Architect Magazine, "Project of the Day, 709 Alton Road", October 2018

The Palm Beach Post, "NEW: FPL unveils plan for 1,000-worker Palm Beach Gardens office amid storm, flood threats", October 2018

Inspicio Arts, "Pat Bosch, Design Director at Perkins&Will", August 2018

Ocean Drive Magazine, "Women on Top of the World", May/June 2018

Africa.com, "Top 10 Greenest Buildings in Africa", Ghana Ridge Hospital, October 2017

Healthcare Design Magazine, "PHOTO TOUR: Nicklaus Children's Hospital Advanced Pediatric Care Pavilion", July 2017

Advisory Board Architectural Design Showcase: "The 21st Design Showcase features 18 ICUs", Nicklaus Children's Hospital, June 2017

Cultured Magazine (culturedmag.com), "The Ring Master", June 2017

CNN Style, Definitive Design, "Hospital Designs That Are Changing the Way You're Cared For" June 2017

Healthcare Design Magazine, "FIRST LOOK: The Center for Obesity and Diabetes", CEMDOE, April 2017

Indulge Magazine, "The Movers - People Who Move Miami", Pat Bosch, April 2017

Architects Newspaper, "Perkins + Will unveils renderings of mixed-use Miami Beach development", 1212 Lincoln Road, April 2017

Health Facilities Magazine, "Miami Children's Health System Expands with New Pediatric Pavilion", March 2017

Miami Today. "Satellite Facilities Changing Ways Healthcare is Delivered" March 2017

Miami Herald, "Perkins + Will Designs For the Future", March 2017

Crain's Miami, "The Latest Trend in Building Design? Bring the Outside In", MDC, March 2017

SunSentinel, "American Express Opens Regional Headquarters in Sunrise", February 2017

Fast Company. "Lessons In Green Building From Africa's First LEED-Certified Hospital" January 2017

Designboom. September 2015 "Construction Begins on Perkins+Will's Ghana Ridge Hospital"

Green Building & Design. July 2015 "Efficiency in Emergency Perkins+Will sustainably designs a Florida International University complex where differing majors spearhead responses to major catastrophies"

Ocean Drive. April, 2015 "Renaissance Woman."

Metropolis. February 19, 2015. "How Do We Design for More Holistic Health-Care Practices?"

Architectural Record. November 11, 2014 "Miami Dade College Student Center and Classroom Complex."

305biz. Fall 2014 "Designing the Future" Hotels.com, Travel Smart Blog. October 9, 2012. "Don't Forget to Look Down"

Huffington Post. September 23, 2011. "Women In Architecture: By Women In Architecture."

New York Times. September 16, 2011 "Hadid to Design A Garage in Miami."

FastCo Design Online, March 11, 2011. "What Starbucks Taught Us About Redesigning College Campuses"

R&D Magazine. December 20, 2010. "Burnham Institute Florida: Green lab seeks cures"

100 Florida Architects and Interior Designers, "Perkins+Will" profile featuring Marlene Liriano and Pat Bosch. 2010

South Florida Business Journal. November 19, 2010. "Miami AIA Chapter's annual competition honors outstanding design"

NCRR Reporter. Fall 2010. "Infusion of Recovery Act Funds Boosts Biomedical Research" features the University of Florida Clinical Translational Research Building

The Gainesville Sun. June 19, 2010. "New Building will help UF boost its clinical research" features the University of Florida Clinical Translational Research Building

Modern Luxury. March 29, 2010

"Architectural Victor: Patricia Bosch" South Florida Design Book, Summer/Fall 2009. "Broader Goals: Perkins+Will's Commitment to Sustainable Design"

South Florida Design Book, March 2009, "Designer Spotlight, Pat Bosch and Marlene Liriano of Perkins+Will"

Architectural Record Schools of the 21st Century, January, 2008, "No One-Size-Fits-All"

Architectural Record Schools of the 21st Century, January 12, 2007, "Central High School - Carroll County Schools"

Miami Today, January 4, 2007, 3333 Biscayne Corridor, "Team of women creating Class A office project on Biscayne Corridor"

Miami Herald, May 13, 2007, "Curves Ahead" Icon at Biscayne, 3333 Biscayne

Miami Herald, June 2006, Victor Hotel

Miami Herald, October 2006, "Fearless Duo" Design Profile of Pat Bosch and Marlene Liriano

Contract Magazine, June 2007 "South Beach Revival" Hotel Victor

Miami Update, Real estate & Lifestyle Magazine Vol. 15 - 2007, "A New Miami

Architectural Icon", 3333 Biscayne Florida Caribbean Architect, June 2006, Miami Beach City Hall Annex Design Award

Florida Caribbean Architect, Fall 2005, Platinum on the Bay, Winner of Unbuilt Honor Award

Florida Trend Magazine, Fall 2006 "Living Large and Green", Platinum on the Bay

Click Press, June 8, 2007, Public Art Competition, 3333 Biscayne, American School and University, Miami Dade College School of Aviation

Miami Herald, August 25, 2002, "MDCC's new Aviation Training Building soars with silvery walls and sleek lines", Miami Dade College School of Aviation

Building Design and Construction, June 2007, "Leading Experts", Academy@998

Home Miami, May 2007, "Revising Rudolph's Riverview"

Palm Beach Post, November 2006, "New Building cements FAU"

Orlando Sentinel, October 3, 2007, "Burnham, UCF medical breakthrough at Lake Nona"

Orlando Sentinel, July 2007, "LEED the way", Burnham Institute for Cancer Research

Florida News, October 2, 2007, "Work starts on Burnham Institute"

Book Credits

Coordination and Research by Jesse Lockwood
Book Layout by Florencia Damilano
Art Direction by Oscar Riera Ojeda
Copy Editing by Kit Maude and Michael W. Phillips Jr.

OSCAR RIERA OJEDA
PUBLISHERS

Copyright © 2023 by Oscar Riera Ojeda Publishers Limited
ISBN 978-1-946226-72-3
Published by Oscar Riera Ojeda Publishers Limited
Printed in China

Oscar Riera Ojeda Publishers Limited
Unit 1331, Beverley Commercial Centre,
87-105 Chatham Road South, Tsim Sha Tsui, Kowloon, Hong Kong

Production Offices
Suit 19, Shenyun Road,
Nanshan District, Shenzhen 518055, China

International Customer Service & Editorial Questions: +1-484-502-5400

www.oropublishers.com | www.oscarrieraojeda.com
oscar@oscarrieraojeda.com

All rights reserved. No part of this book may be reproduced, stored in a retrieval system, or transmitted in any form or by any means, including electronic, mechanical, photo-copying or microfiming, recording, or otherwise (except that copying permitted by Sections 107 and 108 of the U.S. Copyright Law and except by reviewers for the public press) without written permission from the publisher.